Stadium
Progressive Learning

11+ Verbal Reasoning

10 Minute Tests

Shuffled Sentences and Missing Letters — Extra Practice

For ages 10 - 11

Complete preparation
for the 11+ CEM
(Durham University) test

Giving your child the best possible
chance of selection

Studium

Preparing for the 11+ Exam using Studium Books

Preparation for the 11+ exam can be daunting for both students and parents alike.

- Experience tells us that the more a student is prepared, the less nervous they feel on the day. The range of Studium books are expertly designed to support your child's development throughout the months leading up to the exam itself, presenting a range of subjects and authentic question-styles that are likely to be in the exam.

- The tests within this book are designed to improve literacy skills which the 11+ examines. Each test increases in difficulty as your child works through the questions, and throughout the book as a whole, the challenge becomes greater as they develop skills over time.

- Timing each test with a limit of 10 minutes gives a realistic idea of how quickly your child needs to be working.

- A high degree of practice will enable your child to approach the exam with the positive mindset of wanting to show how well they can do, giving themselves the best possible chance of success on the day.

Contents

Studium

11+ Verbal Reasoning — 10 Minute Tests

Questions 1-12: Shuffled Sentences

Reorder the words to create a meaningful sentence.

One word will be superfluous — underline that word.

Set your timer to 10 minutes and try to answer as many questions as you can within the time

1. the past costumes seven musical at starts half

2. a old kitten is opens week its a eyes they when it

3. I the have cupboard my two old from still year in schools books

4. sensible people grow matures more they older become as

5. sea the it looks actually but is transparency blue not

6. one hundred is percent fifth twenty to equal

7. it would find my grandad be to a than difficult nicer mine

8. adding its change adjective a to verb can tense suffix a

9. it have I reading been bed before finished must my book midnight

10. my has a the of house teeth rabbit size friend dog which is a

11. you drained washing water want to until has away might wait the

12. the contained arrived the at wrong it parcel items deliver last but

Questions 13-25: Missing Letters

Fill in the missing letters. Check that your spelling is correct.

Owning a dog can be very **13)re _ _rd _ _ g**. They show

14) _ _ _ ond _ _ional love to their owners and give the

15)w _ _ _ est of greetings when the family **16) _et _ _ ns** home.

It is important that a dog **17)re _ _ _ ves** stimulation such as

playing games and going for walks. This can be fun,

18)es _ec _ _ _ _ ly for children, and does not have to become a

19) _ _ ore. The family could enjoy a **20)str _ _ _** together several

times a week, which would provide good exercise for both

21)h _ _ ans and the canine. At other times, a **22)b _ _ sk** walk

around the local park or along the **23)p _ _eme _ t** would be

appreciated by your four-legged **24)fr _ _ _ d**, who loves nothing

more than to sniff where **25) _ _ her** dogs have been.

/ 25

END OF TEST

Questions 1-12: Shuffled Sentences

Reorder the words to create a meaningful sentence.
One word will be superfluous — underline that word.

Set your timer to 10 minutes and try to answer as many questions as you can within the time

1. my mess chair the always dinner makes at table a brother

2. wish moon rocket the astronaut I fly in a could I to.

3. it must when is homework to do you feel your important alert

4. digest bodies do celery stomach not efficiently human

5. you not irritated hippo can want to annoy a they run as quickly would

6. most the children like on swings running to young play

7. one means partial shape hundred entire percent the

8. you road look before cars must crossing ways the both

9. I our shop day sold so family them I bag eat all sweets wish could

10. the world into the care the without toddler a in splash puddle jumped

11. special can advises be plenty made you warning arrangements of give if

12. you strange keep having as I dolphins am to must to ten pets think want

Questions 13-25: Missing Letters

Fill in the missing letters. Check that your spelling is correct.

My brother has **13)j _ _ _ ed** the town's football club. He is so excited

to be part of the **14) _e _ m** and has already made new

15) _ _ _ ends. They are **16) _ _thus _ _ stic** about football more

than I have ever **17) _ _ow _** ! He and the other players **18)t _ _k**

about it all the time. If they aren't **19)re _al _ _ng** their spectacular

goals, they are **20)dis _ _ssi _ _** who will play in which

21)p _si _ _on, and their tactics to help them gain

22)p _ _ses _ _ on of the ball. I am looking **23)fo _ _ar _**

to seeing them play their next **24) _at _ _** , which is

25)s _ _ _ duled for next Saturday.

/ 25

END OF TEST

Questions 1-12: Shuffled Sentences

Reorder the words to create a meaningful sentence.

One word will be superfluous — underline that word.

Set your timer to 10 minutes and try to answer as many questions as you can within the time

1. the rest are way follow behind of group a long us the

2. half can eight is leave time going the we past latest

3. I to toast my butter burn over before like it cold spread goes

4. the lights and were drivers broken the looked halt traffic confused

5. an beautiful kittens just old puppy dog can as be as a

6. I my hold fifteen breath can seconds dive underwater for

7. I wish brother wanting play we that my was older could together baby so

8. you clover fortunate be of four would to find a leaf

9. the hundreds has thousand five hedgehog between and seven average spikes

10. I wore now year braces a and straight my teeth smile are for

11. arguing back in the driver the distraction car cause a can for road the of

12. my treat and has a for term brother me my we work promised if hard school this condition mum at

Questions 13-25: Missing Letters

Fill in the missing letters. Check that your spelling is correct.

My school has been **13)ta _ k _ _ g** about recycling and how we can help the **14)p _ _ n _ t**. **15)Ap _ _ re _ _ ly**, tonnes of waste plastic have been **16) _ _ _ ped** into the sea and now the **17)w _ _ dl _ _ e** who live there are starting to **18)su _ _ er**. Some animals get their heads stuck in **19)h _ _ es**, and others are eating the small **20)p _ _ _ es** thinking they are bits of **21)fo _ _** . My **22)t _ _ c _ er** said that we need to use less **23)p _ _ kag _ _ g** in the future so that we do not **24)con _ _ nu _ _ ly** cause damage to our **25)w _ _ ld** and those who live in it.

/ 25

END OF TEST

Questions 1-12: Shuffled Sentences

Reorder the words to create a meaningful sentence.

One word will be superfluous — underline that word.

Set your timer to 10 minutes and try to answer as many questions as you can within the time

1. I going am Saturday popcorn that the on we will be to cinema excited

2. be you stirring cook when are hot a pan careful

3. we sale lots of selling money by for favourite raised charity cakes our

4. my fortnight every grandma me to journey school Thursdays takes on

5. sound you not earplugs are if wearing drills goggle loud

6. secondary I looking next meeting forward to am starting September school

7. uncle my trip went a whilst safari abroad observe on

8. it you that winter is during will a cold the months sneeze have likely

9. imagination contemporary when use their artists paint drawing they

10. a can for open only be a limited Sundays time weekend shop on

11. Hetty into back even turning run without to confidently nursery wave walked

12. it a exam take long learn and the skilled able would piano be to take an time to

Questions 13-25: Missing Letters

Fill in the missing letters. Check that your spelling is correct.

Our school **13)lib _ _ ry** is a quiet and peaceful place to visit I like to sit in **14)th _ _ e** after school whilst I am **15)w _ i _ _ ng** for my mum to pick me up, and **16)re _ _** to myself. **17) _ _ _ stly** I read the book that my teacher has set the **18)c _ _ ss**, and then I like to study the **19)at _ _ s** which shows all the countries in the **20) _ _ rl _** . My favourite page shows Australia. It has pictures of **21) _ anga _ _ os** jumping about, and is coloured **22) _ ra _ _ e** and red to show how **23) _ _ t** it is there. My dad says that a lot of Australians **24)ce _ e _ _ ate** Christmas having barbeques on the beach! I would like to **25)e _ _ er _ _ nce** that one day.

/ 25

END OF TEST

Questions 1-12: Shuffled Sentences

Reorder the words to create a meaningful sentence.

One word will be superfluous — underline that word.

Set your timer to 10 minutes and try to answer as many questions as you can within the time

1. you beep the runs stop when time out must writing

2. it cold break in room radiator because my broken is the has

3. as teeth as needles spike puppy sharp are

4. six our bug from were present children school off with a today class stomach

5. test grandma driving month steer her my passed last

6. to percent ten is one greater tenth equal

7. it to behaved have good is when visiting important relatives manners

8. I late might the be as drivers strike have going train on leaves been

9. I to my mum vacuum have when toys wants away to shelves tidy carpet the

10. a invention be that machine would a your correct you homework does for fabulous

11. talented have seeing artists an world way of perceptions amazing the

12. it friends is to two have but is best important it that each converse other like okay they

Questions 13-25: Missing Letters

Fill in the missing letters. Check that your spelling is correct.

Dad and I went fishing last **13)S _ _ _ ay**. It was a warm day, without much **14) _ re _ ze**, and we sat back in our camping chairs, **15)b _ _ _ ing** in the sunshine. Dad is a good conversationalist. We were quietly **16)ch _ _ t _ ng** about all sorts of things when **17)sud _ _ _ ly** the line on my rod started to **18) _ wi _ _ h** and I quickly reeled it in. Success! I hadn't been **19)con _ _ nc _ _** that we would catch anything, but I was pleasantly **20) _ _ rpr _ sed**. Dad took a **21)p _ _ tog _ _ _ h** of me holding my **22) _ _ s _** , and then we let it go back into the **23) _ i _ er**. I want to print the image out and have it in my **24) _ _ d _ oom** to remind me of our lovely **25)t _ _ p**.

/ 25

END OF TEST

Questions 1-12: Shuffled Sentences

Reorder the words to create a meaningful sentence.

One word will be superfluous — underline that word.

Set your timer to 10 minutes and try to answer as many questions as you can within the time

1. think I speaking important that it other to listen people is to

2. my during supervises school grandparents look me the holidays after

3. would be nicer dessert to a than more hard cheesecake find it

4. room I to my every Sunday have tidy cleaning morning

5. my potato vegetables in brother napkin instead his of eating his them hides

6. practice easier my were when I practised every tests day spelling

7. nice vegetable bread improve can slice the of soup taste

8. bought my tickets favourite dad performing me to see live my song singer

9. the sky is moon actually looks stays when same it but it the size bigger low

10. the of pupil assembly looked talking out regretful sent when she was

11. I trying in on the online prefer shops rather buying order clothes than

12. the who their born warm field in February were keep snuggled to lambs mothers

Questions 13-25: Missing Letters

Fill in the missing letters. Check that your spelling is correct.

It will be my **13)** _ _ _ _ **hday** in two weeks and my mum has

14) _ _ _ **mised** me I can have a party. I am still not sure what

I want to **15)** _ **o**. I might ask to go to the soft play **16)a** _ _ **a** in

town, or have friends round **17)** _ _ **ern** _ _ **ht** for a sleepover.

The last sleepover I had was **18)a** _ _ **s** ago, and I did enjoy it very

much. Mum's homemade pizzas were **19)del** _ _ _ **ous**, and we

loved making our own popcorn in the **20)** _ **ac** _ _ **ne**. My friend

Emily thought that it was really **21)f** _ _ **n** _ and the popping

22) _ **o** _ **nd** made her jump. **23)Re** _ _ **mberi** _ _ how fun it was

last **24)t** _ _ **e**, I think I will **25)** _ _ **k** for a sleepover again.

/ 25

END OF TEST

Questions 1-12: Shuffled Sentences

Reorder the words to create a meaningful sentence.

One word will be superfluous — underline that word.

Set your timer to 10 minutes and try to answer as many questions as you can within the time

1. try cooks dinner to finish ready before is homework your

2. I in angry talk please not a good do not to am so mood me

3. equal by eight five is divided forty

4. on are map colouring blue motorways a

5. teacher our will head uncle is with friends my

6. learn collective interesting for nouns are to

7. smart my a is going shoes brother to wearing a older suit party

8. good tea is taste for you like herbal I the cakes but do not

9. my learn teacher has year was me teaching since I in three cello been

10. we characters dressed as literary books our for page from festival up

11. squash end twelve on the castle children once might in bouncy disaster at

12. the was passengers to airport waiting full board their delay of who flights were

Questions 13-25: Missing Letters

Fill in the missing letters. Check that your spelling is correct.

My uncle has decided to run a **13)m _ r _ t _ on**. He is already quite fit and **14) _ _ alt _ y**, but now he has to run twenty six miles, his training **15)pr _ _ _ a _ me** has had to **16) _ n _ rea _ e**. Every morning, he goes out for a gentle jog for five **17) _ _ nu _ es**, followed by thirty minutes of faster **18) _ _ nn _ ng**. It is nice and quiet in the park early in the **19) _ o _ n _ _ g**, although once a dog **20) _ a _ _ ed** at him as he ran past. I don't think it liked his orange hat with the light on which my uncle **21) _ _ ars** so he can see where he is going. I know he has to work **22) _ a _ d** over the next few **23)mo _ _ hs**, but I have **24) _ a _ th** in him that he will **25)su _ _ _ ed**.

/ 25

END OF TEST

Studium

Questions 1-12: Shuffled Sentences

Reorder the words to create a meaningful sentence.

One word will be superfluous — underline that word.

Set your timer to 10 minutes and try to answer as many questions as you can within the time

1. the have cream cakes on pieces best top

2. an often is suffix has adverb a

3. like dressers she my hair I because the friendly cuts lady is who

4. my engine cat like purrs and paws loudly sounds an

5. number odd only is the even two prime

6. it a long take to around time travelling the world would sail

7. can parcel exciting an came for a be experience to arrive waiting

8. dogs chew which paws their needs hair grow trimming between often

9. ground I jumped and somersault in the a the trampoline air immediately on did

10. old been made were patterns pentagonal of leather and footballs black had

11. dolphins groups males pods are and mammals in live social called

12. deputy teacher charge head was in the day the attending head teacher was the left for when absent

Questions 13-25: Missing Letters

Fill in the missing letters. Check that your spelling is correct.

My teacher has **13)d _ _ i _ ed** that we will now have to learn twenty spellings each **14) _ ee _** instead of ten. I am not pleased! She thinks that if we **15) _ _ a _ n** more words, our English work will **16)i _ _ ro _ e**. My parents **17)a _ _ ee** with her, and have told me I need to **18)pr _ _ t _ _ e** every day. So last night I **19)be _ _ n** the new plan and spent ages saying the **20) _ et _ _ rs** to my dog, as she was the only one who didn't mind **21)l _ _ _ ening**. I am **22)be _ _ _ ning** to think that doing a little bit of work every day is a good **23)i _ _ a**, and I will try to **24) _ ee _** it up. I really want to get good **25) _ _ ore _** in my tests.

/ 25

END OF TEST

Studium

Questions 1-12: Shuffled Sentences

Reorder the words to create a meaningful sentence.

One word will be superfluous — underline that word.

Set your timer to 10 minutes and try to answer as many questions as you can within the time

1. the were the brought when barn snowed cows was into it

2. drinking drinks is good your for brush teeth sugary not

3. tail baby fabulous would a to dragon own a pet be

4. quarter half fifty is hundred of one

5. I pods peas eating when mixed rice are but with not like they

6. fly is rain it to birds sky lower going when

7. I let everyone was would a party boss work office if I the have at

8. our front heated car in the wheels has seats new

9. I not going sparkle shopping it do look on like is toys nice the to at Saturdays but

10. have games better stopped since behaved concentration been you playing video you

11. people itchy have eczema rash experience and who uncomfortable skin often

12. most much using are of phone the aware of technology dangers too teenagers

Questions 13-25: Missing Letters

Fill in the missing letters. Check that your spelling is correct.

On our recent camping **13)** _ _ **ip**, I learnt how to make beans on

14)t _ a _ t. Dad wanted to create an **15)** _ _ **thent** _ _ bonfire

but Mum insisted on doing things **16)sen** _ _ _ **ly** and got out the

portable stove **17)** _ _ _ **tead**. I learnt that we needed to

18)t _ _ **n** the bread over after one **19)** _ _ **nu** _ **e**, and make sure

it didn't start to burn on the **20)** _ _ **ge** _ . I needed to wear an

oven glove and had to be **21)** _ _ _ **e** _ **ul** when using the metal

utensil. The beans bubbled a little bit in the **22)** _ _ **n** then I

23) _ _ **ur** _ **d** them on top of the **24)** _ _ _ **st**.

My meal was really **25)** _ **ast** _ !

/ 25

END OF TEST

Questions 1-12: Shuffled Sentences

Reorder the words to create a meaningful sentence.

One word will be superfluous — underline that word.

Set your timer to 10 minutes and try to answer as many questions as you can within the time

1. the patiently in room waited the seat family waiting

2. dog my underneath grass walk take when we her for a bushes sniffs

3. your always hands food wash chop before preparing

4. left we so have must quick minutes hurry five only

5. I reached success in target maths have for term my this

6. we go out dinner on for breakfast always a roast Sundays

7. there four which are at forgot of I school types learnt noun have

8. add times is seventy eight bigger nine than

9. leaf vegetables good strange green you quite are look for but

10. brother food always his spits moans tired then it my out he's chews when

11. I a machine do that to want do all the design I don't will want to helps things

12. I spending in the room on I beanbag prefer to my like library time although sitting read

Questions 13-25: Missing Letters

Fill in the missing letters. Check that your spelling is correct.

My grandparents will be taking me to see a **13) _ _ ay** at the theatre on Saturday. I know that my grandad's **14) _ _ _ our _ te** actor will take the lead **15)r _ _ e**. There will also be an actor there whom I have seen **16) _ e _ ore**. I hope that **17) _ _ is** time I will get to **18) _ e _ t** him at the end and ask for his

19) _ _ togra _ h. The **20)pe _ _ orma _ _ e** will

21) _ om _ _ n _ e at half past seven. I am expected to

22)d _ e _ _ smartly for the **23) _ _ casion**, and have chosen to

24) _ _ ar my favourite shiny **25) _ h _ e _** .

/ 25

END OF TEST

Studium

Questions 1-12: Shuffled Sentences

Reorder the words to create a meaningful sentence.
One word will be superfluous — underline that word.

Set your timer to 10 minutes and try to answer as many questions as you can within the time

1. you striving best always your hardest try must do and your

2. patient line please in orderly wait an

3. our cloudy trip it the rained all museum day to was fun but

4. Christmas many on celebrate beach barbeque Australians the

5. I pleased your achievements you of hope proud are that

6. my been heard listening clearly have concerns

7. rest eaten of tomorrow picnic the remain lunch can for be the

8. ferrets many enjoy around letting the house hiding people their run

9. four two is to squared halve times equal eight

10. I ankle down since have with had I startled the stairs problems fell my

11. you want the interested theatre are in reaction join performing might to group you if

12. a ship carry height on a twenty can a maximum approximately of kilograms container cargo weight thousand

Questions 13-25: Missing Letters

Fill in the missing letters. Check that your spelling is correct.

The old **13)l _ _ y** who lives **14)a _ _ o _ s** the road from our house

has just **15) _ _ opted** two cats. She used to have three dogs at one

16) _ i _ e, but as she has **17) _ ro _ n** older, she has become

18)in _ _ pa _ _ e of holding them back when they pull on the

19)l _ a _ . It would be terrible if an **20)a _ _ i _ _ nt** happened

because the lady was not **21) _ _ ron _** enough to take

22) _ _ ar _ e of her dogs, so it is a good idea for her to have cats

23) _ _ stea _ . Cats do not need to be taken out on walks — instead

they will curl up next to her on cold, **24) _ _ nte _** nights and be

cuddly **25)c _ _ pa _ i _ ns** in the house.

/ 25

END OF TEST

Questions 1-12: Shuffled Sentences

Reorder the words to create a meaningful sentence.

One word will be superfluous — underline that word.

Set your timer to 10 minutes and try to answer as many questions as you can within the time

1. I twins lucky friend am my loyal very that best is

2. day I very winter look that exciting think sports

3. leave to I a today in might bit early little have

4. dentist into climb smiles at I as chair my teeth me the

5. the village different in attend a school other my places children

6. strange house that heard ghost in noises been derelict have

7. park full had the car was so to the street driving park on we

8. apples than peel have ones that taste been raw cooked stronger

9. was night I jump that over I dreamt clouds last the leaping

10. is maps to your most so the of time it plan make important the can holiday you

11. a monitoring can alongside to humans help dog unconditionally work trained and them be

12. my wants to me on her camping but I a tent my sister distraction join trip find might

Questions 13-25: Missing Letters

Fill in the missing letters. Check that your spelling is correct.

My first ever **13) _ _ t** was a goldfish in a little **14) _ an _** . I loved him very much and used to watch him swim around between the **15) _ _ as _ ic** plants and model **16)c _ _ t _ e** on top of the stones. I **17) _ _ gre _** to say that my little friend did not have a **18) _ a _ e**. I used to **19)re _ _ _** to him as 'the fish' so that my family knew who I was talking about, but now I am older I **20) _ _ _ lise** that every pet needs a name because it shows how much you **21) _ _ re**. My **22)n _ _ t** pet will also be a fish, but this **23)ti _ _** I want a clownfish to make me laugh. He will have a **24) _ am _** this time, but I am yet to **25)de _ i _ e** what it will be.

/ 25

END OF TEST

Questions 1-12: Shuffled Sentences

Reorder the words to create a meaningful sentence.

One word will be superfluous — underline that word.

Set your timer to 10 minutes and try to answer as many questions as you can within the time

1. the villain finally emerged in the was caught story

2. I my dog my sleep curl was to bed wish allowed on

3. teacher instructions sounds when gives my voice swimming loud she

4. you have get to soon your well pen so surprising done licence

5. a red rainbow bring do rain to like people who not can joy

6. is very mistakes nice to of wish out others it point not the

7. shine decorated I that my be year in brightly this bedroom paint will coloured hope

8. hours we after airport Australia a of six in finally delay arrived

9. I started lessons and to part have the sing dancing want in contest take talent

10. my grandchildren youngest grandad I grow seven am has the and

11. mum's roses all my are of flowers like petal but not the smell I favourite do

12. album sweet old looking might you think at of looked I you like photographs but not yourself

Questions 13-25: Missing Letters

Fill in the missing letters. Check that your spelling is correct.

Some people have lovely **13)ne _ _ _ bo _ rs**, but others are not that

14) _ _ cky. The **15) _ am _ _ y** living next **16) _ _ or** to us are noisy

and very **17) _ es _ y**. Their garden is full of rubbish that needed to

be **18)th _ o _ n** away months ago. Once, when I **19) _ _ ered** over

the **20) _ _ nc _** , I could see an old pushchair looking very

21)r _ s _ y. There were black **22) _ _ gs** full of broken objects and

next to them was a **23)k _ _ ch _ n** sink with the tap still

24)a _ _ a _ _ ed. My dad is **25) _ _ _ si _ ering** going-round

to offer help.

/ 25

END OF TEST

Questions 1-12: Shuffled Sentences

Reorder the words to create a meaningful sentence.

One word will be superfluous — underline that word.

Set your timer to 10 minutes and try to answer as many questions as you can within the time

1. multiply maths know if you your times easier is tables

2. it is paste teeth to your before clean bed go important to you

3. please ignore whilst stay me I the results wait with for

4. a can word a to prefix mean side change the opposite

5. slices delicious are sauce of but banana strawberries loathe I

6. my drive sister is she confident very is not yet down learning but to

7. already passing I am about trip packed my our have and bags excited

8. my ride horses soon cousin to has a and I it pony hope

9. of a lot for plastics young toys primary children are decorated colours in

10. be pigs dogs football trained can and to kick play both

11. planet rotate ago scientists that was Earth believe over billion four and a formed half years

12. mountaineers have rucksack fit be might to the to struggle they very mountain otherwise ascend

Questions 13-25: Missing Letters

Fill in the missing letters. Check that your spelling is correct.

At the **13)** _ **eg** _ _ _ **ing** of March, it was very **14)** _ _ **ld**.
We'd had snow during **15)Feb** _ _ _ **ry** and the roads were still
quite **16)sl** _ **p** _ _ **ry**. My grandma **17)st** _ _ **gg** _ **es** to walk on
icy **18)p** _ _ **eme** _ _ **s** to get to the shop, so my dad had been
taking her in the car and helping her buy **19)e** _ _ **ent** _ **als**. With
all of this positive **20)** _ _ **tention**, my grandma had got used to
the help. Now she **21)rea** _ _ **s** _ **s** that she is quite lonely living a
22)so _ _ **ta** _ **y** life in her **23)bu** _ _ _ **low**, and wants to move in
with us. There is **24)s** _ _ **ce** for her in the spare room, and I think
she will be **25)a** _ **r** _ _ **ing** shortly.

/ 25

END OF TEST

Questions 1-12: Shuffled Sentences

Reorder the words to create a meaningful sentence.

One word will be superfluous — underline that word.

Set your timer to 10 minutes and try to answer as many questions as you can within the time

1. the wrong driver was directions nice drove but he way coach very the

2. important swim pool it how learns is every to that child

3. team success good work project a helps succeed to

4. enclosures has my mum a snake scared but the of neighbours pet are it

5. use check remaining answers the your look to time

6. I my trousers dad a for wears bought his work birthday and he tie it to

7. snow travel I love to London it is in would when visit covered

8. if away tidy smartly you your toys then each the will house look day nicer

9. the according tiles of an the pool can outdoor to weather temperature vary

10. most teachers watch are effective child listening every when is

11. enjoyed I still dislocating our sports shot-put day sling the my with school despite finger

12. would I enjoy my like ideal bowling party but be to record day singing a star myself pop birthday

Questions 13-25: Missing Letters

Fill in the missing letters. Check that your spelling is correct.

I used to have a hot **13)di _ _ e _** at school every

14)l _ n _ ht _ me, but recently I have **15) _ _ _ nged** my mind and I

now take sandwiches and a piece of **16) _ _ u _ _** . The problem

17)o _ _ u _ _ ed about a week ago when my friend Sam was

18) _ _ ti _ g his custard. It looked nice and it smelt **19) _ _ _ my**, but

when he tried it, he **20)rea _ _ _ ed** there was a lump inside. He used

his spoon to prod it and **21)p _ _ e** it, but he could not

22) _ _ entify what it was. The dinner lady didn't know and

neither did the **23) _ _ ok**. So he **24) _ _ _ hed** his tray away

with a look of **25)di _ _ ust** on his face, and neither he nor I have

eaten a hot dinner since.

/ 25

END OF TEST

Questions 1-12: Shuffled Sentences

Reorder the words to create a meaningful sentence.

One word will be superfluous — underline that word.

Set your timer to 10 minutes and try to answer as many questions as you can within the time

1. I a lot of starting friends new have since my school bag made

2. I out think ten getting that nine achievement is an scores of

3. teachers exercise home over to have many mark weekend the books

4. sixty lot notes a of pounds money five is

5. regional my weekends plays sister football for team the

6. my century seventy are years grandparents old both

7. shout many sound very barking together loud dogs can

8. Christmas father people is expensive time many an year for of

9. I Sunday a event attend half of month the running every third

10. know are begins your tired you when stare you to wane concentration

11. contains a thermometer readings high can give as fifty low minus degrees mercury as and

12. best racquet will play friend for joining summer a my during the and I am tennis considering him club

Questions 13-25: Missing Letters

Fill in the missing letters. Check that your spelling is correct.

When I grow up, I want to be an **13)en _ _ n _ _ r**. I like fixing

machines that are **14)br _ _ en**, such as the alarm clock

15)b _ _ on _ _ ng to my sister which **16)co _ _ inua _ _ y** rang every

hour until it was **17)sw _ _ _ hed** off. I know I will have to study

18) _ _ _ ence and maths when I'm older. I enjoy maths at

19) _ c _ _ ol at the **20)m _ _ en _** , and my teacher says I am

21)e _ _ ee _ _ ng expectations. I like to talk about mechanical

things with my uncle, who spends his **22)we _ _ e _ ds** building

machines out of **23) _ _ rap** metal. If I get stuck with my

24) _ ome _ or _ , I can always ask him. He is very **25)cl _ _ er.**

/ 25

END OF TEST

Studium

Questions 1-12: Shuffled Sentences

Reorder the words to create a meaningful sentence.

One word will be superfluous — underline that word.

Set your timer to 10 minutes and try to answer as many questions as you can within the time

1. day am looking I forward trip our year to residential next

2. may tracks to make check you the train want just to sure times again

3. their mower during gardeners the gardens autumn plan

4. I tables my to times thirteen subtract know up

5. a cat walk a would collar strange but fun be taking for

6. have cake balloons I a big at my I birthday hope tomorrow party

7. twelve a you a are bread dozen baker makes unless

8. pies always taste so part lovely picnic have pork as blanket of a we them

9. grateful I be say if being could without wash your hands would asked you

10. rewarded Daniel of commitment sessions attended for certificate his was all training the and

11. sugar my with favourite is icing torte and a of whip lemon pudding cream sprinkling

12. measured greatness better by succeed is by failures you success overcome immediate than

Questions 13-25: Missing Letters

Fill in the missing letters. Check that your spelling is correct.

My little **13)s _ _ _ er** has learnt how to walk. She is

14)le _ _ than a year old, and people are **15)sa _ _ ng** that she

has **16)d _ _ elo _ ed** more quickly than **17)e _ _ ec _ ed**.

I don't know if this **18)i _ _ lies** that she will be **19) _ a _ able** in

everything she tries in the **20) _ u _ ure**; we will find out as she

grows **21) _ _ der**. At the **22)mo _ _ nt**, I am very **23) _ rou _** of

her and I like to **24) _ _ ow** her off to people we **25) _ ee _** .

/ 25

END OF TEST

Questions 1-12: Shuffled Sentences

Reorder the words to create a meaningful sentence.

One word will be superfluous — underline that word.

Set your timer to 10 minutes and try to answer as many questions as you can within the time

1. you party pizza tomatoes need one a than more for

2. that you do box don't ask open whatever

3. my a good roast seriously dad taste dinner makes

4. my perhaps planning me grandma choose will help

5. pain it I have broke in since I eyelash had arm my

6. more flowers beautiful sunshine in leaf look the

7. a dog third an has more eyes one teeth fully-grown adult than human

8. wedding ring so place the takes in city had take centre the better the we train

9. it unlikely is it happened it snow in but that has break before March will

10. our down elderly each is dry able to up of day terrier grams crunch food seventy still

11. only go which Charlie to the them won match the with two scored minute goal one

12. bough the fall in conserve weather survive autumn so its and water wintry leaves tree each supply can

Questions 13-25: Missing Letters

Fill in the missing letters. Check that your spelling is correct.

At school this term, we are learning about **13)ri _ e _ s** and mountains. The topic sounds very **14)i _ _ erest _ ng** and I feel **15)e _ _ ited**. So far we have had to try to **16) _ ma _ ine** how tall some of the world's **17)t _ _ les _** mountains are, which has blown my mind! I **18)a _ _ ire** the **19) _ ountain _ _ _ s** who attempt to climb to these **20)h _ _ ghts**, and I worry whether they will **21)s _ _ vi _ e** if there is an avalanche. For our homework, we have to make a **22)m _ _ el** of a mountain, showing the shape of the **23) _ _ aks** and using paint to **24)ind _ _ _ te** rock and snow. We have six weeks to **25) _ _ _ plete** it.

/ 25

END OF TEST

Studium

Questions 1-12: Shuffled Sentences

Reorder the words to create a meaningful sentence.

One word will be superfluous — underline that word.

Set your timer to 10 minutes and try to answer as many questions as you can within the time

1. mammal a hedgehog a snuffle is spiny

2. my increased money as grown I has younger have older pocket

3. have colour three ducks vision eyelids feet and

4. fish salt and taste and shop vinegar them with chips better on

5. hair it to a take Nick get seems long ready to time

6. rely shops on charity of from donations general fundraise public clothes the

7. I the that my of I like are text can fact a different variety so things teachers learn

8. whistle pitch can referees use blown a be heard across they the entire so

9. my son mum's uncle husband sister's is

10. was anniversary of yesterday marriage the celebrate neighbour's my

11. avoided fortunately is good my accident a driver and an dad having crash

12. many Eastertime the go Southern because Europe people too at can summer in feel it cream hot to

Questions 13-25: Missing Letters

Fill in the missing letters. Check that your spelling is correct.

My dad works as a lecturer in a **13)un _ _ ers _ _ y**. He has to teach
the **14) _ _ ude _ ts** there, but **15)in _ _ _ _ d** of it being like school
where the **16) _ _ il _ _ en** put their **17) _ _ nds** up and
18) _ _ s _ _ r, they all just sit there and listen — for **19) _ _ urs**.
I don't think I could listen to my dad for that long, even if I had to.
He likes to use **20)c _ m _ _ icated** words that are hard to
21)un _ _ rsta _ d, and he goes into so much **22)de _ _ il** I forget the
23)to _ i _ after a while. I know my dad has worked really hard and I
have been told that his job **24)i _ _ erv _ _ ws** were quite difficult, so
I am very **25) _ _ oud** of him.

$$/\,25$$

END OF TEST

Questions 1-12: Shuffled Sentences

Reorder the words to create a meaningful sentence.

One word will be superfluous — underline that word.

Set your timer to 10 minutes and try to answer as many questions as you can within the time

1. divided is six two take by twelve

2. never I seen ants have an eater until eating ant

3. sufficient the be fixed surely can computer

4. will six be o'clock at tennis once serve dinner we from practice home are

5. I parrot I could around lose my to school wish classroom take and fly it the let

6. horse I love own a too but would to my feed mum is expensive says it

7. I started have you take and twice out the four asked rubbish it smell to now to has

8. under found Tim search cushion his was for all and them morning a keys eventually looking

9. rabbits pet each fifty day eat grate grams of added dry carrots food in with my

10. pin early board get we the next train to must each seats to other enough

11. there clear is a you route chance get woods a through the lost would without boots

12. who part bore take in thrill like people often feel the of to danger sports extreme

Questions 13-25: Missing Letters

Fill in the missing letters. Check that your spelling is correct.

I tried to make **13)b _ _ akfa _ t** by myself at the weekend. I thought it would be a good **14) _ _ ea** to boil some eggs, make some toast and **15) _ _ d** a drink of orange juice. To start with, I **16)st _ _ g _ l _ d** to get the eggs from the fridge, so I stood on a chair and reached high up to the shelf, just about **17)g _ i _ _ ing** the box. As I stretched, the chair slipped and I started to fall. **18)L _ _ _ ily** I landed on my feet but the egg box fell from my hand onto the floor and all the eggs cracked, **19)c _ _ at _ _ g** a sticky mess which **20)d _ _ pe _ _ ed** in all directions. I then tried to make some toast but it burnt, **21)tr _ _ _ ering** the smoke alarm to **22)de _ _ eni _ _ ly** beep. The orange juice was almost **23) _ uc _ _ _ _ fully** in the glass when mum **24)in _ al _ d** with exasperation and I knew I was in **25) _ _ ou _ _ e.**

/ 25

END OF TEST

Questions 1-12: Shuffled Sentences

Reorder the words to create a meaningful sentence.

One word will be superfluous — underline that word.

Set your timer to 10 minutes and try to answer as many questions as you can within the time

1. band I playing the pianos enjoy saxophone the school in

2. camping I wait the and next cannot until fire year loved trip

3. you ill you become when healthily eat are older easy if might you do not

4. it time a looking the long our to rescue earn of dog took trust

5. being can pace down affect you your and tired concentration slow

6. sister my started without little has on swimming her towel armbands

7. I was be would jolt it shocking if so upset not

8. summertime animals hard heat find it to water cope the of the in

9. Christmas Mum vegetables in the every prepares advance lettuce Eve

10. worst about watch thing having a programmes sister is to babyish cry younger having the

11. park a dog your get is good for health air you and different people meet walking because fresh some

12. eyesight eagles eight have times four than talon to more human effective vision

Questions 13-25: Missing Letters

Fill in the missing letters. Check that your spelling is correct.

My dad's **13)colle _ _ u _** at work has decided to **14) _ _ igra _ e** to America. He has only lived in this **15)c _ _ nt _ y** for four years, but now he **16) _ _ els** ready to move on again. I don't know where he grew up, but I think his **17)a _ _ ent** sounds a little bit like the German **18) _ an _ u _ g _** . My dad doesn't speak any **19) _ _ re _ _ n** languages, so they always speak in English, but I know that there is a **20)t _ an _ _ at _ r** working within their **21)co _ _ an _** who could've helped if they had needed it. I think my dad will **22)m _ _ s** him when he moves **23)a _ ro _ d**, as I know they enjoy having interesting **24) _ on _ ers _ tio _ s** during their lunch break, and sharing stories about their **25) _ _ mi _ y** holidays.

/ 25

END OF TEST

Questions 1-12: Shuffled Sentences

Reorder the words to create a meaningful sentence.

One word will be superfluous — underline that word.

Set your timer to 10 minutes and try to answer as many questions as you can within the time

1. a drums name drake male is the duck of a

2. is anniversary my today babysitter's of calling the wedding

3. species of live the seventeen ocean world hedgehog throughout

4. you chance dessert will be able vegetables not to a if you not your have do eat

5. an over rabbit can eagle see flew kilometres a in away a three field from

6. too threat motorists a lorry a to cyclist can many pose

7. a story easy finish is words knowing challenge to starting but how it be a can

8. a lot of be items are which thrown could such away dispose recycled

9. the crops had the farmer started before to tractor it gather raining

10. you cat want to the groom bath herself let shampoo rather give might her than a

11. was the that ten teacher out achieved improved class concerned one in had ten of no the

12. the net referee ball look to at whether the to confirm offside the was footage had video

Studium

Questions 13-25: Missing Letters

Fill in the missing letters. Check that your spelling is correct.

Next term, our class will go on a **13)re _ ide _ _ i _ l** trip for three days. We are all very excited about it, and are **14)c _ _ re _ _ ly** deciding who will share a **15)d _ _ m _ _ ory**. My first choices would be Nicky and Jo, who are my best friends, but the **16) _ _ a _ her** has told us that she cannot **17)g _ _ ran _ _ e** we will be given our **18) _ _ _ fer _ _ ce**. Many girls are still **19)un _ _ c _ _ ed** at the moment, and some have had **20) _ _ arrels** because they cannot be **21)c _ _ ar** on who they want. I think the **22)s _ _ _ f** may have to **23)c _ _ at _** the groups themselves and **24)s _ lec _** children at **25) _ an _ o _** to share a room.

/ 25

END OF TEST

Questions 1-12: Shuffled Sentences

Reorder the words to create a meaningful sentence.

One word will be superfluous — underline that word.

Set your timer to 10 minutes and try to answer as many questions as you can within the time

1. has years ankle slip it three I been broke my since

2. pleased although happier changed I that I much and am I feel schools now

3. commitment a learning instrument hard enthusiastic can musical much work take and

4. join I fortnight want to scouts the and on adventures them go with

5. you have taking once only nine live but lives cats

6. Sasha surpass of a film club joined becoming dreamt the local star and drama

7. Lizzie match three and elated goals the trophy for player of the scored the awarded being all was

8. a spying head bird has vision all and can excellent almost round the its see way

9. I holiday entertain in our enjoyed Asian I visiting prefer although countries Spain

10. groups people movements swim fit the use lessons many because muscle who are

11. helpful hedgehogs garden are to nocturnal are not owners whereas animals other evenings

12. score that low wrong corrections was then I taken but I had the paper upsetting realised

Studium

Questions 13-25: Missing Letters

Fill in the missing letters. Check that your spelling is correct.

Our trip to the safari park was an **13)u _ _ er** disaster! On the journey there, my grandma felt **14)n _ _ seou _** because of the motion of the car, and my little brother **15)scr _ _ me _** with excitement which gave Mum a **16) _ _ ad _ _ he**. Once we got onto the **17)pr _ _ ises**, there were so many cars. It would have been **18)un _ _ _ e** to overtake the other **19)v _ _ icl _ s** because the **20)an _ ma _ _** were so close to the road. So we sat behind a large people **21) _ _ rri _ r** for what seemed like an **22)e _ _ r _ _ ty**, and our car **23)e _ _ in _** overheated. The park **24)r _ _ gers** towed us out of the **25)en _ _ os _ _ e** to the safety of the grey carpark.

/ 25

END OF TEST

Questions 1-12: Shuffled Sentences

Reorder the words to create a meaningful sentence.

One word will be superfluous — underline that word.

Set your timer to 10 minutes and try to answer as many questions as you can within the time

1. one twelve is subtract forty squared and four hundred

2. forward I am excited out to looking my trying new the park in skateboard

3. feel my happy main in others is laugh life to and make challenges aim

4. sweets within save you prefer your might party to until the after

5. tell it difficult to is look they when confide off cute someone

6. wanted time since park I tiger have a visited pet the we safari

7. completing the will rest the of class test silence the be

8. human sixty brainy of about water body the overall percent is

9. reached the would target soon small made be could if a donation everyone

10. a fruit badger from of the foot will a during tree night reveals the take

11. have days always grate you good but nice they happen are cannot they when

12. school whether teacher wonder my I reception still at me is the working same

Questions 13-25: Missing Letters

Fill in the missing letters. Check that your spelling is correct.

For a career, I am **13)co _ _ ide _ _ ng** becoming a

14)j _ _ rna _ _ st. I love hearing about the events in other people's

lives, both **15)l _ _ all _** and from around the **16) _ _ obe**, so it

makes perfect **17) _ _ _ se** that I might one day be reporting on them

myself. There are different **18) _ _ pes** of reporters, from those who

19)c _ _ me _ _ on the royal **20)fa _ _ ly** to those in war

21)z _ _ _ s where **22)c _ _ fl _ _ t** is rife. Maybe the best way to

23)s _ _ rt would be to write for the school **24) _ _ wslet _ _ r**, and

see whether others **25) _ _ pr _ _ e**.

/ 25

END OF TEST

Questions 1-12: Shuffled Sentences

Reorder the words to create a meaningful sentence.

One word will be superfluous — underline that word.

Set your timer to 10 minutes and try to answer as many questions as you can within the time

1. study to I go become to might medicine to university want

2. will a give for word inspect a synonyms chosen thesaurus many

3. transparent efficient most catch moist the place the to mole is hedgerow a under

4. adjust it a while abroad on to takes refrain heat the to you go holiday when

5. might be influx this cycle buses weekend to race due the delayed

6. Antarctica abroad ducks hundreds live but are living the in no in sea there

7. a can determine be high windsock in flown the wind air to the minimise direction of the

8. the confetti ringing village church started bells the were across the wedding ceremony before

9. we netball trophy believed practised chance stood our we a of winning until skills we

10. it early is go a good to morning without can so you function the fully to in idea bed

11. playing my field suggestion hockey of on rapidly the in dejected snow the was rejected

12. hurting have broke if my would already not wasn't bad shoulder so it sore been

Questions 13-25: Missing Letters

Fill in the missing letters. Check that your spelling is correct.

I often **13)w _ _ de _** what is inside the wooden **14)tr _ _ _** under my parents' bed. Whenever I have **15)hi _ _ ed** that I am **16)c _ r _ _ us**, they deny all **17) _ _ owle _ g _** of it being there, and instead try to **18) _ i _ _ ract** me with **19) _ _ scu _ _ ions** about school. I know I am **20) _ or _ _ _ den** from knowing what it **21) _ _ nta _ ns**, which makes my **22) _ _ _ iosi _ y** grow even more. Perhaps they will **23) _ _ v _ lge** the information when I am considered **24)m _ t _ _ e** enough to learn their **25)pr _ _ i _ _ s** secrets.

/ 25

END OF TEST

Answers

Shuffled Sentences & Missing Letters:
10 MINUTE TESTS

The sentence created by the student may be different to that given here in terms of structure or punctuation. This is acceptable on the condition that coherency and meaning remain the same.

FOR EXAMPLE:

'Last week, my mum went to see a play' has the same meaning and coherency as *'My mum went to see a play last week'*, although the sentence structure and punctuation differ. Similarly, *'Ten is half of twenty'* is equivalent to *'Half of twenty is ten'.*

One mark should be given for identifying the correct superfluous word.

TEST: ONE

1. **costumes** – The musical starts at half past seven.

2. **they** – A kitten opens its eyes when it is a week old.

3. **schools** – I still have my old books from year two in the cupboard.

4. **matures** – People become more sensible as they grow older.

5. **transparency** – The sea looks blue but actually it is not.

6. **hundred** – Twenty percent is equal to one fifth.

7. **my** – It would be difficult to find a nicer grandad than mine.

8. **adjective** – Adding a suffix to a verb can change its tense.

9. **bed** – It must have been midnight before I finished reading my book.

10. **teeth** – My friend has a house rabbit which is the size of a dog.

11. **washing** – You might want to wait until the water has drained away.

12. **deliver** – The parcel arrived at last but it contained the wrong items.

13. rewarding

14. unconditional

15. warmest

16. returns

Shuffled Sentences & Missing Letters:
10 MINUTE TESTS

17. receives

18. especially

19. chore

20. stroll

21. humans

22. brisk

23. pavement

24. friend

25. other

TEST: TWO

1. **chair** – My brother always makes a mess at the dinner table.

2. **astronaut** – I wish I could fly to the moon in a rocket.

3. **must** – It is important to do your homework when you feel alert.

4. **stomach** – Human bodies do not digest celery efficiently.

5. **irritated** – You would not want to annoy a hippo as they can run quickly.

6. **running** – Most young children like to play on the swings.

7. **partial** – One hundred percent means the entire shape.

8. **cars** – You must look both ways before crossing the road.

9. **bag** – I wish our family shop sold sweets so I could eat them all day.

10. **splash** – The toddler jumped into the puddle without a care in the world.

11. **advises** – Special arrangements can be made if you give plenty of warning.

12. **having** – You must think I am strange to want to keep ten dolphins as pets.

13. joined

14. team

15. friends

16. enthusiastic

17. known

18. talk

19. recalling

Shuffled Sentences & Missing Letters:
10 MINUTE TESTS

20. discussing

21. position

22. possession

23. forward

24. match

25. scheduled

TEST: THREE

1. **follow** – The rest of the group are a long way behind us.

2. **going** – Half past eight is the latest time we can leave.

3. **burn** – I like to spread butter over my toast before it goes cold.

4. **halt** – The traffic lights were broken and the drivers looked confused.

5. **kittens** – An old dog can be just as beautiful as a puppy.

6. **dive** – I can hold my breath underwater for fifteen seconds.

7. **wanting** – I wish that my baby brother was older so we could play together.

8. **of** – You would be fortunate to find a four leaf clover.

9. **hundreds** – The average hedgehog has between five and seven thousand spikes.

10. **smile** – I wore braces for a year and now my teeth are straight.

11. **road** – Arguing in the back of the car can cause a distraction for the driver.

12. **condition** – My mum has promised a treat for me and my brother if we work hard at school this term.

13. talking

14. planet

15. apparently

16. dumped

17. wildlife

18. suffer

19. holes

20. pieces

21. food

22. teacher

Shuffled Sentences & Missing Letters:
10 MINUTE TESTS

23. packaging

24. continually

25. world

TEST: FOUR

1. **popcorn** – I am excited that we will be going to the cinema on Saturday.

2. **cook** – Be careful when you are stirring a hot pan.

3. **sale** – We raised lots of money for our favourite charity by selling cakes.

4. **journey** – My grandma takes me to school every fortnight on Thursdays.

5. **goggle** – Drills sound loud if you are not wearing earplugs.

6. **meeting** – I am looking forward to starting secondary school next September.

7. **observe** – My uncle went on a safari trip whilst abroad.

8. **sneeze** – It is likely that you will have a cold during the winter months.

9. **drawing** – Contemporary artists use their imagination when they paint.

10. **weekend** – A shop can only be open for a limited time on Sundays.

11. **run** – Hetty walked confidently into nursery without even turning back to wave.

12. **skilled** – It would take a long time to learn the piano and be able to take an exam.

13. library

14. there

15. waiting

16. read

17. firstly

18. class

19. atlas

20. world

21. kangaroos

22. orange

23. hot

Answers

Shuffled Sentences & Missing Letters:
10 MINUTE TESTS

24. celebrate

25. experience

TEST: FIVE

1. **beep** – You must stop writing when the time runs out.

2. **break** – It is cold in my room because the radiator has broken.

3. **spike** – Puppy teeth are as sharp as needles.

4. **present** – Six children from our class were off school with a stomach bug today.

5. **steer** – My grandma passed her driving test last month.

6. **greater** – Ten percent is equal to one tenth.

7. **behaved** – It is important to have good manners when visiting relatives.

8. **leaves** – I might be late as the train drivers have been going on strike.

9. **shelves** – I have to tidy my toys away when mum wants to vacuum the carpet.

10. **correct** – A fabulous invention would be a machine that does your homework for you.

11. **perceptions** – Talented artists have an amazing way of seeing the world.

12. **converse** – It is okay to have two best friends but it is important that they like each other.

13. Sunday

14. breeze

15. basking

16. chatting

17. suddenly

18. twitch

19. convinced

20. surprised

21. photograph

22. fish

23. river

24. bedroom

25. trip

Shuffled Sentences & Missing Letters:
10 MINUTE TESTS

TEST: SIX

1. **speaking** – I think that it is important to listen to other people.

2. **supervises** – My grandparents look after me during the school holidays.

3. **more** – It would be hard to find a nicer dessert than cheesecake.

4. **cleaning** – I have to tidy my room every Sunday morning.

5. **potato** – My brother hides his vegetables in his napkin instead of eating them.

6. **practice** – My spelling tests were easier when I practised every day.

7. **slice** – Nice bread can improve the taste of vegetable soup.

8. **song** – My dad bought me tickets to see my favourite singer performing live.

9. **sky** – The moon looks bigger when it is low but actually it stays the same size.

10. **talking** – The pupil looked regretful when she was sent out of assembly.

11. **order** – I prefer trying on clothes in the shops rather than buying online.

12. **field** – The lambs who were born in February snuggled their mothers to keep warm.

13. birthday

14. promised

15. do

16. area

17. overnight

18. ages

19. delicious

20. machine

21. funny

22. sound

23. remembering

24. time

25. ask

Answers

Shuffled Sentences & Missing Letters:
10 MINUTE TESTS

TEST: SEVEN

1. **cooks** – Try to finish your homework before dinner is ready.

2. **angry** – I am not in a good mood so please do not talk to me.

3. **equal** – Forty divided by five is eight.

4. **colouring** – Motorways are blue on a map.

5. **will** – Our head teacher is friends with my uncle.

6. **for** – Collective nouns are interesting to learn.

7. **shoes** – My older brother is going to a party wearing a smart suit.

8. **cakes** – Herbal tea is good for you but I do not like the taste.

9. **learn** – My cello teacher has been teaching me since I was in year three.

10. **page** – We dressed up as characters from books for our literary festival.

11. **squash** – Twelve children on the bouncy castle at once might end in disaster.

12. **delay** – The airport was full of passengers who were waiting to board their flights.

13. marathon

14. healthy

15. programme

16. increase

17. minutes

18. running

19. morning

20. barked

21. wears

22. hard

23. months

24. faith

25. succeed

Answers

Studium

Shuffled Sentences & Missing Letters:
10 MINUTE TESTS

TEST: EIGHT

1. **pieces** – The best cakes have cream on top.

2. **is** – An adverb often has a suffix.

3. **dressers** – I like the lady who cuts my hair because she is friendly.

4. **paws** – My cat purrs loudly and sounds like an engine.

5. **odd** – Two is the only even prime number.

6. **travelling** – It would take a long time to sail around the world.

7. **came** – Waiting for a parcel to arrive can be an exciting experience.

8. **chew** – Dogs grow hair between their paws which often needs trimming.

9. **ground** – I immediately jumped on the trampoline and did a somersault in the air.

10. **been** – Old footballs were made of leather and had black pentagonal patterns.

11. **males** – Dolphins are mammals and live in social groups called pods.

12. **attending** – The deputy head teacher was left in charge for the day when the head teacher was absent.

13. decided

14. week

15. learn

16. improve

17. agree

18. practise

19. began

20. letters

21. listening

22. beginning

23. idea

24. keep

25. scores

Answers

Shuffled Sentences & Missing Letters:
10 MINUTE TESTS

TEST: NINE

1. **was** – The cows were brought into the barn when it snowed.

2. **brush** – Drinking sugary drinks is not good for your teeth.

3. **tail** – A baby dragon would be a fabulous pet to own.

4. **quarter** – Fifty is half of one hundred.

5. **pods** – I like eating peas but not when they are mixed with rice.

6. **sky** – Birds fly lower when it is going to rain.

7. **office** – I would let everyone have a party at work if I was the boss.

8. **wheels** – Our new car has heated seats in the front.

9. **sparkle** – I do not like going shopping on Saturdays but it is nice to look at the toys.

10. **concentration** – You have been better behaved since you stopped playing video games.

11. **rash** – People who have eczema often experience itchy and uncomfortable skin.

12. **phone** – Most teenagers are aware of the dangers of using technology too much.

13. trip

14. toast

15. authentic

16. sensibly

17. instead

18. turn

19. minute

20. edges

21. careful

22. pan

23. poured

24. toast

25. tasty

Shuffled Sentences & Missing Letters:
10 MINUTE TESTS

TEST: TEN

1. **seat** – The family waited patiently in the waiting room.

2. **grass** – My dog sniffs underneath bushes when we take her for a walk.

3. **chop** – Always wash your hands before preparing food.

4. **quick** – We only have five minutes left so must hurry.

5. **success** – I have reached my target in maths for this term.

6. **breakfast** – We always go out for a roast dinner on Sundays.

7. **forgot** – There are four types of noun which I have learnt at school.

8. **add** – Nine times eight is bigger than seventy.

9. **leaf** – Green vegetables are good for you but look quite strange.

10. **moans** – My brother always chews his food then spits it out when he's tired.

11. **helps** – I want to design a machine that will do all the things I don't want to do.

12. **room** – I like spending time in the library although I prefer to read sitting on my beanbag.

13. play

14. favourite

15. role

16. before

17. this

18. meet

19. autograph

20. performance

21. commence

22. dress

23. occasion

24. wear

25. shoes

Shuffled Sentences & Missing Letters:
10 MINUTE TESTS

TEST: ELEVEN

1. **striving** – You must always try your hardest and do your best.

2. **patient** – Please wait in an orderly line.

3. **cloudy** – Our trip to the museum was fun but it rained all day.

4. **barbeque** – Many Australians celebrate Christmas on the beach.

5. **pleased** – I hope that you are proud of your achievements.

6. **listening** – My concerns have been clearly heard.

7. **remain** – The rest of the picnic can be eaten tomorrow for lunch.

8. **hiding** – Many people enjoy letting their ferrets run around the house.

9. **halve** – Two times eight is equal to four squared.

10. **startled** – I have had problems with my ankle since I fell down the stairs.

11. **reaction** – You might want to join the theatre group if you are interested in performing.

12. **height** – A container on a cargo ship can carry a maximum weight of approximately twenty thousand kilograms.

13. lady

14. across

15. adopted

16. time

17. grown

18. incapable

19. lead

20. accident

21. strong

22. charge

23. instead

24. winter

25. companions

Answers

Shuffled Sentences & Missing Letters:
10 MINUTE TESTS

TEST: TWELVE

1. **twins** – I am very lucky that my best friend is loyal.

2. **day** – I think that winter sports look very exciting.

3. **in** – I might have to leave a little bit early today.

4. **teeth** – My dentist smiles at me as I climb into the chair.

5. **places** – The other children in my village attend a different school.

6. **ghost** – Strange noises have been heard in that derelict house.

7. **driving** – The car park was full so we had to park on the street.

8. **peel** – Raw apples taste stronger than ones that have been cooked.

9. **jump** – Last night I dreamt that I was leaping over the clouds.

10. **maps** – It is important to plan your holiday so you can make the most of the time.

11. **monitoring** – A dog can be trained to work alongside humans and help them unconditionally.

12. **tent** – My sister wants to join me on my camping trip but I might find her a distraction.

13. pet

14. tank

15. plastic

16. castle

17. regret

18. name

19. refer

20. realise

21. care

22. next

23. time

24. name

25. decide

Shuffled Sentences & Missing Letters:
10 MINUTE TESTS

TEST: THIRTEEN

1. **emerged** – The villain in the story was finally caught.

2. **curl** – I wish my dog was allowed to sleep on my bed.

3. **voice** – My swimming teacher sounds loud when she gives instructions.

4. **surprising** – You have done well to get your pen licence so soon.

5. **red** – A rainbow can bring joy to people who do not like rain.

6. **wish** – It is not very nice to point out the mistakes of others.

7. **shine** – I hope that my bedroom will be decorated in brightly coloured paint this year.

8. **airport** – We finally arrived in Australia after a delay of six hours.

9. **sing** – I have started dancing lessons and want to take part in the talent contest.

10. **grow** – My grandad has seven grandchildren and I am the youngest.

11. **petal** – Roses are my mum's favourite of all flowers but I do not like the smell.

12. **album** – You might not like looking at old photographs of yourself but I think you looked sweet.

13. neighbours

14. lucky

15. family

16. door

17. messy

18. thrown

19. peered

20. fence

21. rusty

22. bags

23. kitchen

24. attached

25. considering

Answers

Studium

Shuffled Sentences & Missing Letters:
10 MINUTE TESTS

TEST: FOURTEEN

1. **multiply** – Maths is easier if you know your times tables.

2. **paste** – It is important to clean your teeth before you go to bed.

3. **ignore** – Please stay with me whilst I wait for the results.

4. **side** – A prefix can change a word to mean the opposite.

5. **sauce** – Strawberries are delicious but I loathe slices of banana.

6. **down** – My sister is learning to drive but she is not very confident yet.

7. **passing** – I have already packed my bags and am excited about our trip.

8. **horses** – My cousin has a pony and I hope to ride it soon.

9. **plastics** – A lot of toys for young children are decorated in primary colours.

10. **kick** – Pigs and dogs can both be trained to play football.

11. **rotate** – Scientists believe that planet Earth was formed over four and a half billion years ago.

12. **rucksack** – Mountaineers have to be very fit otherwise they might struggle to ascend the mountain.

13. beginning

14. cold

15. February

16. slippery

17. struggles

18. pavements

19. essentials

20. attention

21. realises

22. solitary

23. bungalow

24. space

25. arriving

Answers

Studium

Shuffled Sentences & Missing Letters:
10 MINUTE TESTS

TEST: FIFTEEN

1. **directions** – The coach driver was very nice but he drove the wrong way.

2. **pool** – It is important that every child learns how to swim.

3. **success** – Good team work helps a project to succeed.

4. **enclosures** – My mum has a pet snake but the neighbours are scared of it.

5. **look** – Use the remaining time to check your answers.

6. **trousers** – I bought my dad a tie for his birthday and he wears it to work.

7. **travel** – I would love to visit London when it is covered in snow.

8. **smartly** – If you tidy away your toys each day then the house will look nicer.

9. **tiles** – The temperature of an outdoor pool can vary according to the weather.

10. **watch** – Teachers are most effective when every child is listening.

11. **sling** – I still enjoyed our school sports day despite dislocating my finger with the shotput.

12. **day** – I enjoy bowling but my ideal birthday party would be to record myself singing like a pop star.

13. dinner

14. lunchtime

15. changed

16. fruit

17. occurred

18. eating

19. yummy

20. realised

21. poke

22. identify

23. cook

24. pushed

25. disgust

Shuffled Sentences & Missing Letters:
10 MINUTE TESTS

TEST: SIXTEEN

1. **bag** – I have made a lot of friends since starting my new school.

2. **scores** – I think that getting nine out of ten is an achievement.

3. **home** – Many teachers have to mark exercise books over the weekend.

4. **notes** – Sixty five pounds is a lot of money.

5. **weekends** – My sister plays football for the regional team.

6. **century** – My grandparents are both seventy years old.

7. **shout** – Many dogs barking together can sound very loud.

8. **father** – Christmas is an expensive time of year for many people.

9. **half** – I attend a running event every third Sunday of the month.

10. **stare** – You know you are tired when your concentration begins to wane.

11. **high** – A thermometer contains mercury and can give readings as low as minus fifty degrees.

12. **racquet** – My best friend will play for a tennis club during the summer and I am considering joining him.

13. engineer

14. broken

15. belonging

16. continually

17. switched

18. science

19. school

20. moment

21. exceeding

22. weekends

23. scrap

24. homework

25. clever

Answers

Shuffled Sentences & Missing Letters:
10 MINUTE TESTS

TEST: SEVENTEEN

1. **day** – I am looking forward to our residential trip next year.

2. **tracks** – You may want to check the train times again just to make sure.

3. **mower** – Gardeners plan their gardens during the autumn.

4. **subtract** – I know my times tables up to thirteen.

5. **collar** – Taking a cat for a walk would be strange but fun.

6. **balloons** – I hope I have a big cake at my birthday party tomorrow.

7. **bread** – Twelve makes a dozen unless you are a baker.

8. **blanket** – Pork pies taste lovely so we always have them as part of a picnic.

9. **say** – I would be grateful if you could wash your hands without being asked.

10. **certificate** – Daniel attended all of the training sessions and was rewarded for his commitment.

11. **whip** – My favourite pudding is lemon torte with cream and a sprinkling of icing sugar.

12. **succeed** – Greatness is better measured by failures you overcome than by immediate success.

13. sister

14. less

15. saying

16. developed

17. expected

18. implies

19. capable

20. future

21. older

22. moment

23. proud

24. show

25. meet

Answers

Studium

Shuffled Sentences & Missing Letters:
10 MINUTE TESTS

TEST: EIGHTEEN

1. **tomatoes** – You need more than one pizza for a party.

2. **ask** – Whatever you do don't open that box.

3. **taste** – My dad makes a seriously good roast dinner.

4. **planning** – Perhaps my grandma will help me choose.

5. **eyelash** – I have had pain in my arm since I broke it.

6. **leaf** – Flowers look more beautiful in the sunshine.

7. **eyes** – A fully–grown dog has one third more teeth than an adult human.

8. **ring** – The wedding takes place in the city centre so we had better take the train.

9. **break** – It is unlikely that it will snow in March but it has happened before.

10. **down** – Our elderly terrier is still able to crunch up seventy grams of dry food each day.

11. **two** – With only one minute to go, Charlie scored the goal which won them the match.

12. **bough** – Leaves fall in the autumn so each tree can conserve its water supply and survive wintry weather.

13. rivers

14. interesting

15. excited

16. imagine

17. tallest

18. admire

19. mountaineers

20. heights

21. survive

22. model

23. peaks

24. indicate

25. complete

Shuffled Sentences & Missing Letters:
10 MINUTE TESTS

TEST: NINETEEN

1. **snuffle** – A hedgehog is a spiny mammal.

2. **younger** – My pocket money has increased as I have grown older.

3. **feet** – Ducks have colour vision and three eyelids.

4. **shop** – Fish and chips taste better with salt and vinegar on them.

5. **hair** – It seems to take Nick a long time to get ready.

6. **fundraise** – Charity shops rely on donations of clothes from the general public.

7. **text** – I like the fact that my teachers are different so I can learn a variety of things.

8. **blown** – Referees use a whistle so they can be heard across the entire pitch.

9. **son** – Mum's sister's husband is my uncle.

10. **celebrate** – Yesterday was the anniversary of my neighbour's marriage.

11. **crash** – Fortunately my dad is a good driver and avoided having an accident.

12. **cream** – Many people go to Southern Europe at Eastertime because it can feel too hot in the summer.

13. university

14. students

15. instead

16. children

17. hands

18. answer

19. hours

20. complicated

21. understand

22. detail

23. topic

24. interviews

25. proud

Shuffled Sentences & Missing Letters:
10 MINUTE TESTS

TEST: TWENTY

1. **take** – Twelve divided by six is two.

2. **until** – I have never seen an ant eater eating ants.

3. **sufficient** – Surely the computer can be fixed.

4. **serve** – Dinner will be at six o'clock once we are home from tennis practice.

5. **lose** – I wish I could take my parrot to school and let it fly around the classroom.

6. **feed** – I would love to own a horse but my mum says it is too expensive.

7. **four** – I have asked you twice to take out the rubbish and now it has started to smell.

8. **search** – Tim was looking for his keys all morning and eventually found them under a cushion.

9. **grate** – Each day my pet rabbits eat fifty grams of dry food with carrots added in.

10. **pin** – We must board the train early enough to get seats next to each other.

11. **boots** – There is a chance you would get lost without a clear route through the woods.

12. **bore** – People who take part in extreme sports often like to feel the thrill of danger.

13. breakfast

14. idea

15. add

16. struggled

17. gripping

18. luckily

19. creating

20. dispersed

21. triggering

22. deafeningly

23. successfully

24. inhaled

25. trouble

Shuffled Sentences & Missing Letters:
10 MINUTE TESTS

TEST: TWENTY ONE

1. **pianos** – I enjoy playing the saxophone in the school band.

2. **fire** – I loved the camping trip and cannot wait until next year.

3. **easy** – You might become ill when you are older if you do not eat healthily.

4. **looking** – It took a long time to earn the trust of our rescue dog.

5. **pace** – Being tired can affect your concentration and slow you down.

6. **towel** – My little sister has started swimming without her armbands on.

7. **jolt** – I would be upset if it was not so shocking.

8. **water** – Animals find it hard to cope in the heat of the summertime.

9. **lettuce** – Mum prepares the vegetables in advance every Christmas Eve.

10. **cry** – The worst thing about having a younger sister is having to watch babyish programmes.

11. **park** – Walking a dog is good for your health because you get some fresh air and meet different people.

12. **talon** – Eagles have eyesight four to eight times more effective than human vision.

13. colleague

14. emigrate

15. country

16. feels

17. accent

18. language

19. foreign

20. translator

21. company

22. miss

23. abroad

24. conversations

25. family

Answers

Shuffled Sentences & Missing Letters:
10 MINUTE TESTS

TEST: TWENTY TWO

1. **drums** – A drake is the name of a male duck.

2. **calling** – Today is the anniversary of my babysitter's wedding.

3. **ocean** – Seventeen species of hedgehog live throughout the world.

4. **chance** – You will not be able to have a dessert if you do not eat your vegetables.

5. **flew** – An eagle can see a rabbit in a field from over three kilometres away.

6. **lorry** – Too many motorists can pose a threat to a cyclist.

7. **words** – Starting a story is easy but knowing how to finish it can be a challenge.

8. **dispose** – Such a lot of items are thrown away which could be recycled.

9. **tractor** – The farmer had to gather the crops before it started raining.

10. **shampoo** – You might want to let the cat groom herself rather than give her a bath.

11. **improved** – The teacher was concerned that no one in the class had achieved ten out of ten.

12. **net** – The referee had to look at the video footage to confirm whether the ball was offside.

13. residential

14. currently

15. dormitory

16. teacher

17. guarantee

18. preference

19. undecided

20. quarrels

21. clear

22. staff

23. create

24. select

25. random

Shuffled Sentences & Missing Letters:
10 MINUTE TESTS

TEST: TWENTY THREE

1. **slip** – It has been three years since I broke my ankle.

2. **although** – I am pleased that I changed schools and now I feel much happier.

3. **enthusiastic** – Learning a musical instrument can take much hard work and commitment.

4. **fortnight** – I want to join the scouts and go on adventures with them.

5. **taking** – You only live once but cats have nine lives.

6. **surpass** – Sasha dreamt of becoming a film star and joined the local drama club.

7. **elated** – Lizzie scored all three goals and was awarded the trophy for being the player of the match.

8. **spying** – A bird has excellent vision and can see almost all the way round its head.

9. **entertain** – I enjoyed our holiday in Spain although I prefer visiting Asian countries.

10. **lessons** – People who swim are fit because the movements use many muscle groups.

11. **evenings** – Hedgehogs are helpful to garden owners whereas other nocturnal animals are not.

12. **corrections** – That low score was upsetting but then I realised I had taken the wrong paper.

13. utter

14. nauseous

15. screamed

16. headache

17. premises

18. unsafe

19. vehicles

20. animals

21. carrier

22. eternity

23. engine

24. rangers

25. enclosure

Answers

Shuffled Sentences & Missing Letters:
10 MINUTE TESTS

TEST: TWENTY FOUR

1. **subtract** - Twelve squared is one hundred and forty four.

2. **excited** - I am looking forward to trying out my new skateboard in the park.

3. **challenges** - My main aim in life is to make others laugh and feel happy.

4. **within** - You might prefer to save your sweets until after the party.

5. **confide** - It is difficult to tell someone off when they look cute.

6. **time** - I have wanted a pet tiger since we visited the safari park.

7. **silence** - The rest of the class will be completing the test.

8. **brainy** - About sixty percent of the human body overall is water.

9. **could** - The target would soon be reached if everyone made a small donation.

10. **reveals** - A badger will take fruit from the foot of a tree during the night.

11. **grate** - You cannot always have good days but they are nice when they happen.

12. **me** - I wonder whether my reception teacher is still working at the same school.

13. considering

14. journalist

15. locally

16. globe

17. sense

18. types

19. comment

20. family

21. zones

22. conflict

23. start

24. newsletter

25. approve

Shuffled Sentences & Missing Letters:
10 MINUTE TESTS

TEST: TWENTY FIVE

1. **become** - I might want to go to university to study medicine.

2. **inspect** - A thesaurus will give many synonyms for a chosen word.

3. **transparent** - The most efficient place to catch a mole is under the moist hedgerow.

4. **refrain** - It takes a while to adjust to the heat when you go on holiday abroad.

5. **influx** - Buses might be delayed this weekend due to the cycle race.

6. **aboard** - No ducks live in Antarctica but there are hundreds living in the sea.

7. **minimise** - A windsock can be flown high in the air to determine the direction of the wind.

8. **confetti** - The church bells were ringing across the village before the wedding ceremony started.

9. **trophy** - We practised our netball skills until we believed we stood a chance of winning.

10. **without** - It is a good idea to go to bed early so you can fully function in the morning.

11. **dejected** - My suggestion of playing hockey on the field in the snow was rapidly rejected.

12. **broke** - Hurting my shoulder would not have been so bad if it wasn't already sore.

13. wonder

14. trunk

15. hinted

16. curious

17. knowledge

18. distract

19. discussions

20. forbidden

21. contains

22. curiosity

23. divulge

24. mature

25. precious

 # Notes

 **Notes**